This book belongs to:

_____

BUTT ARTIST

What can **you** draw with a **butt?**

Everything!

everything
butt art

on the FARM

You can bring a
farm to life using
your imagination,
some **creativity**
and...

(a butt)

Always start with a **butt!**

1

2

The pink lines show you what to add in each step.

3

4

5

6

The **farm**
is full of
hidden butts.

See how many you can
find in a game of **Butt Hunt!**

Unlike most animals, a horse wears shoes. Did you know people play a game with horseshoes? Imagine if a horse played a game with your shoes!

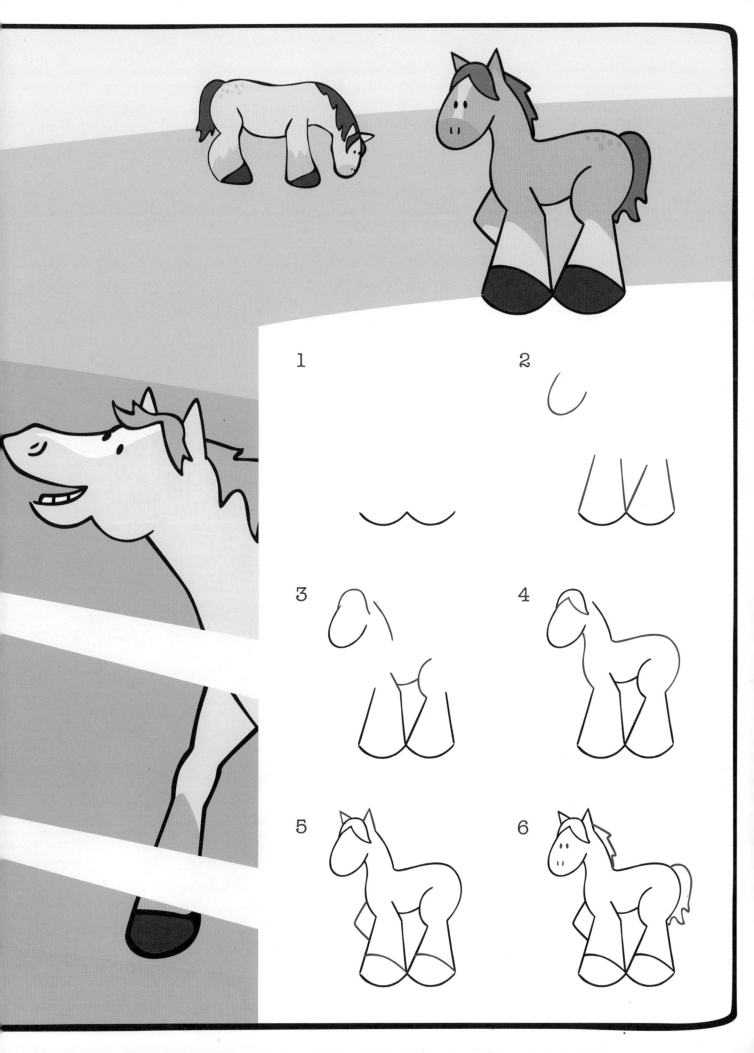

1

2

3

4

5

6

Is waking the farmer with his cock-a-doodle-doo the rooster's most important squawk of the day? Probably not. With so many predators nearby, he's very serious about warning the flock of danger.

1

2

3

4

5

6

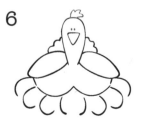

While goats are said to eat just about anything, apparently their taste in beverages is more refined. Some say they discovered coffee.

Cream and sugar, please!

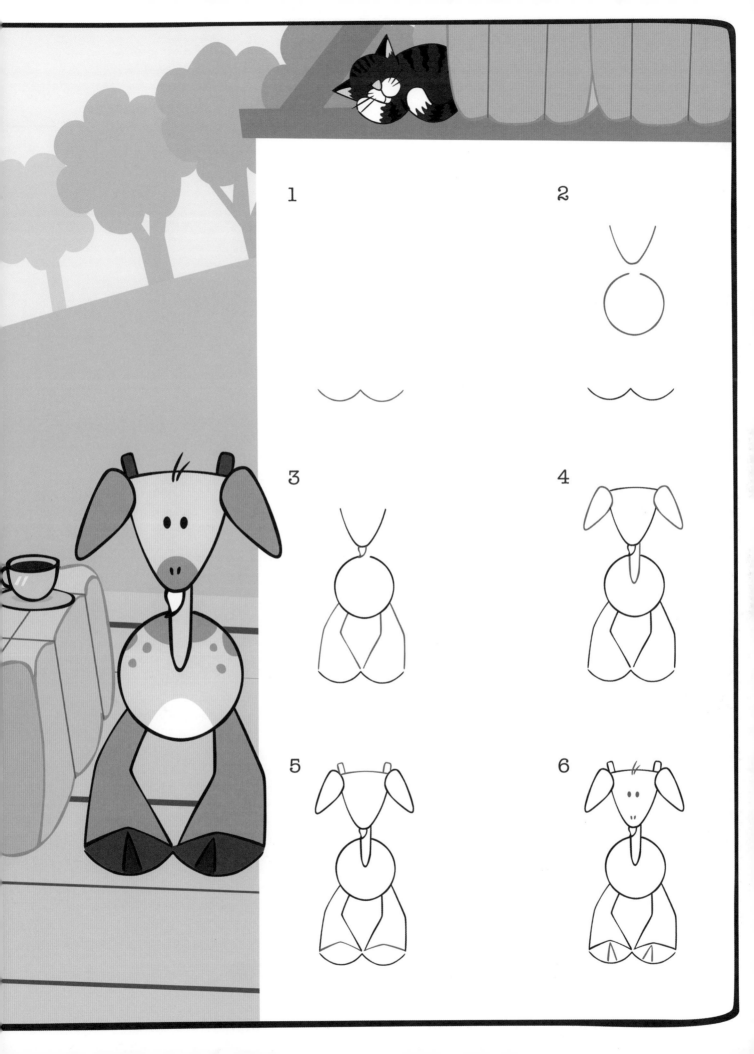

1

2

3

4

5

6

A llama can be a friendly travel companion. He'll even help carry your stuff. But, don't overload him. An overburdened llama is an unhappy llama. He'll lie down, refuse to move, and maybe even hiss, spit, or kick.

pssssst

1

2

3

4

5

6

BARN

Can you find all the barn-related words?
They appear sideways, upside-down, downside-up,
backwards, forwards and diagonally, too!

```
E R U K O R E D I P S U S P
W A G O N E I A G I C A I I
P E R U N A M Z S T A L L G
I L A V I W I T U C G C O W
E D I T T J O P O H Z O N O
U D N R H A Y L O F T E A I
G A O A E E B H G O N I E T
L S E C T X R O H R A E C F
A Y N T A U A V I K O D H V
X E T O W K J Y A E E B I P
F M S R U I E R T N I A C A
T G A F E C L A J Z E L K B
M I C E Y A R X O S H E E P
B U C K E T W U L B E D N Q
```

chicken
silo
grain
bucket
mice
spider
weathervane
pitchfork
hayloft
bale
cow
pig
goat
rat
cat
saddle
tractor
wagon
manure
sheep
fence
stall

Can you spot the differences between these two barn cats?

1

2

3

4

5

6

An apple a day keeps the doctor away. What about the dentist? With 44 teeth in an adult pig's mouth, she's got twelve more teeth than an adult human.

Say, "Ahhh!"

1

2

3

4

5

6

Meow!

House cats have it easy. They lie in the sun, curl up next to the fireplace, and enjoy food served to them. For barn cats, life isn't so luxurious. They only eat if they do their job - catching rodents on the farm. Which cat would you prefer to be?

Where did all the cheese go?

+KITCHEN

BARN→

How did the rat get into the farmer's kitchen? He probably chewed his way in. Rats can gnaw through wood, concrete, and even metal. This helps them gain access to places off-limits to other animals.

FARMHOUSE

_____ _____ _____ _____ _____

No one knows which of these came first. Decode the answer using the key below.

Connect the dots to reveal the farmer's favorite pet. It looks like the housecat is jealous.

1

2

3

4

5

6

Sheepdogs got their name by herding and protecting sheep. But, because of its herding instinct, a sheepdog may also try to herd children. Do you think he would try to herd you?

1

Start with two butts this time!

2

3

4

5

6

1

2

3

4

5

6

Pillow fight!

After flying thousands of miles, geese trade in their old, worn feathers and grow new ones. That's called molting. What do you think happens to all those old feathers? Do they end up in goose down pillows?

Holy cow!
That's a lot of milk.

An average dairy cow produces almost 100 glasses of milk per day. It's a good thing she makes so much because yummy things like ice cream, yogurt, and cheese are made from milk.

Burp!

Uh oh, someone had too much ice cream!

1

2

3

4

5

6

Color this cow by number
with the flower key.

Use the clues below to fill in
the pasture-themed crossword.

ACROSS

4. no need to mow this when you have cows around
5. equine
6. one with four leaves is lucky
7. where farm animals graze
8. a horse younger than one year old
10. a group of horses

DOWN

1. ground cover of plants
2. baby cow
3. eat in a pasture
5. only eat plant-based foods
6. another name for cows
9. a young sheep

What a useful machine! A tractor is used to plow, plant, and harvest fields. However, its best job is pulling a hayride. Have you been on a hayride?

All aboard!

1

2

3

4

5

6

A rabbit nibbles to keep her teeth the right length. Otherwise, her teeth will keep growing and growing and growing. Would anyone like a carrot to nibble?

1

2

3

4

5

6

1
2
3
4
5
6

In a vegetable garden, a big mound of fresh soil often means a gopher has moved in. Typically unwelcome, he can be quite destructive. Digging tunnels and stealing vegetables, a gopher can single-handedly ruin a garden. Where's that barn cat?

Scarecrows often, but not always, resemble humans. Regardless of their form, they all have the same task – to scare away birds that will damage the crop. Does this scarecrow look like he's doing a good job?

1

2

3

4

5

6

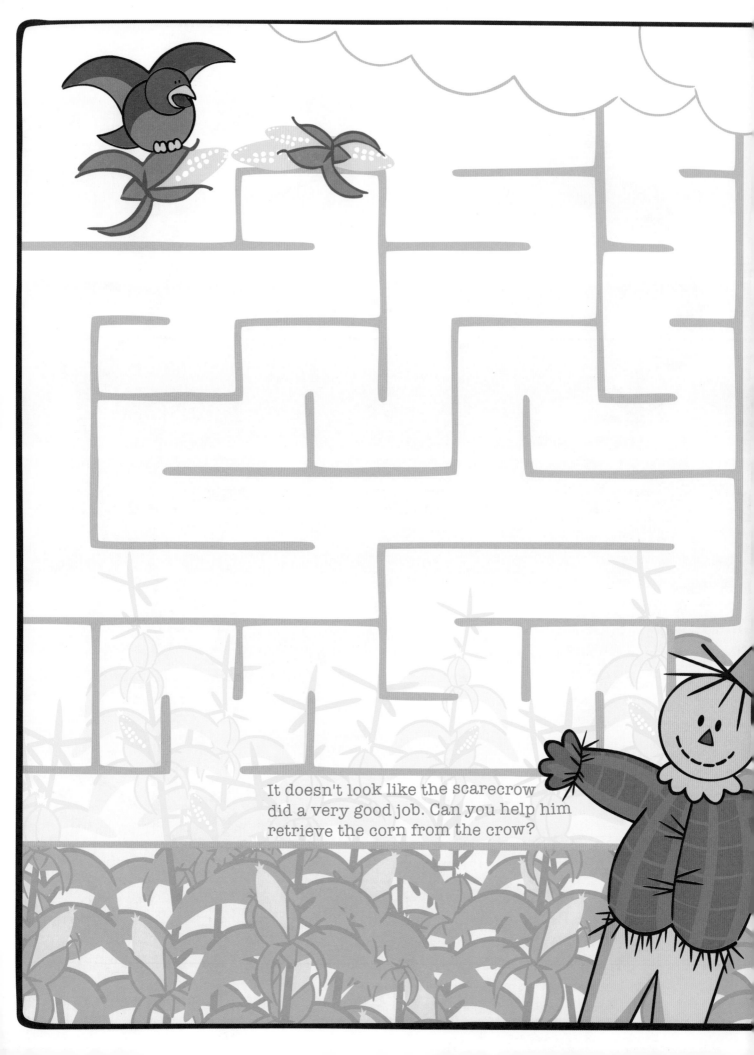

It doesn't look like the scarecrow did a very good job. Can you help him retrieve the corn from the crow?

CORNFIELD

Unscramble the names of things you find in a cornfield.

WACCERSOR _____

KUSH ____

RENKLE _____

LOIS ____

VARTHES _____

ROCN ____

LIATARUGUCE _____

PROC ____

NIRAG _____

CATRORT _____

answers

BARN

FARMHOUSE

chicken

or egg

answers

PASTURE

Crossword answers:
- vegetation
- calf
- grass
- grazе
- horse
- herbivore
- clover
- cattle
- pasture
- herd
- foal
- lamb

CORNFIELD

WACCERSOR <u>scarecrow</u>

KUSH <u>husk</u>

RENKLE <u>kernel</u>

LOIS <u>soil</u>

VARTHES <u>harvest</u>

ROCN <u>corn</u>

IATARUGUCE <u>agriculture</u>

PROC <u>crop</u>

NIRAG <u>grain</u>

CATRORT <u>tractor</u>

FSC
MIX
FSC® C002614

This book's cover is made from 50% post-consumer recycled paper.

The interior pages are made from 100% FSC certified eucalyptus fibers.

Using recycled paper saved 4 trees and 1,748 gallons of waste water!

(find our full environmental audit online)

Mmmm, eucalyptus!

3,250 copies printed in Twinsburg, Ohio by Oliver Printing Company.